YOUR BUSINESS PLAN

A Workbook For Owners of Small Businesses

Dennis J. Sargent, CPA

Maynard Chambers

Chris Pryor

4th Edition

Oregon Small Business Development Center Network
44 West Broadway, Suite 501
Eugene, OR 97401-3021

ISBN 1-878475-05-3

Preface

This workbook was written by Dennis Sargent, Maynard Chambers, and Chris Pryor for publication and distribution by the Oregon Small Business Development Center Network. The workbook is designed for those investigating the possibility of opening their first business, as well as business owners with many years of experience who have never prepared a written business plan.

The development of a written business plan, sometimes called a feasibility study or financing proposal, is a critical but often overlooked step in the management of a small business. This workbook will guide you through the process of preparing your business plan.

The materials presented here are a result of working with thousands of aspiring and existing business owners. We wish to thank the business owners we have worked with, the Small Business Development Center directors, and Small Business Management instructors throughout Oregon for their valuable input.

Dennis Sargent is the chairman of the Training and Business Development Center at Linn-Benton Community College. He worked in a variety of positions in the private sector for ten years prior to coming to LBCC. His experience includes working in the consulting division of an international CPA firm, actuarial experience for a national insurance company, and two management positions in private industry.

Maynard Chambers was Chairman of the Business Management Department at Linn-Benton Community College from 1970 to 1990 and currently teaches accounting and finance courses at the college. He worked in a variety of managerial positions in the electrical contracting industry prior to coming to LBCC and was active in the early years of the Oregon Small Business Development Center Network

Chris Pryor is Marketing Supervisor for the Willamalane Park & Recreation District in Springfield, Oregon. His responsibilities include marketing research, strategic planning and promotional development and implementation. Pryor has experience working with both public and private organizations. He conducts seminars and workshops on marketing and advertising throughout the state and serves as president of the Southwest Oregon Chapter of the American Marketing Association.

Good luck with your plan and your business!

Table of Contents

How to Use the Workbook

The workbook should be used step by step from front to back. The sections should be completed in the order presented to obtain maximum benefit from the workbook approach. A suggested method for completing your business plan is given below.

Step 1: Read workbook quickly to get a "feel" for its layout.

Step 2: Read workbook carefully but do not fill in the blanks.

Step 3: Identify sections that meet your needs.

Determine which sections you need to complete to accomplish your purpose. You may want outside assistance in making this determination. If you obtained your copy at your local Small Business Development Center office, ask a counselor at the office to help you select the sections you need. Indicate selected sections by placing check marks in front of section names in the table of contents.

Step 4: Attempt exercises and work sheets in proper order.

Time to pick up your pencil and go to work! You should not expect to complete the workbook on your first attempt. Keep a list of information you will need to research in order to complete the workbook, but do as much as you can the first time through.

The workbook can be viewed as a series of exercises and work sheets that will result in your completed business plan. Instructions are on the left-hand pages as you look at the open workbook and exercises or work sheets are on the right-hand pages. The instructions consist of numbered steps-just like this page–often with questions to help you understand what information is required. Answers may be written on both pages but the information on the right-hand page will go into your completed business plan.

Step 5: Research needed information to complete the plan.

Step 6: Complete the workbook.

Step 7: Assemble completed business plan.

Your completed business plan should consist of pages from this workbook assembled in the order shown on the next page. Your completed plan will not contain all the pages listed but, rather, only the sections you selected in Step 3.

Business Plan Outline

* If you are preparing your business plan for a time period longer than one year, these pages should be repeated for each year.

Importance of Planning

Why should you go to all the work of completing this workbook?

Here are eight reasons the process will be worth your time and effort:

1) The thinking involved in answering the questions posed in this workbook will force you to take a thorough look at your whole business rather than focusing on an individual aspect.

2) The completed workbook can be a feasibility study to help you evaluate a new business idea or a business plan to ensure the continued success of an existing business.

3) The completed workbook will be a tool to help you better manage your daily business operations more successfully.

4) The completed workbook will help you communicate your business ideas to persons outside your business and can be used as a financing proposal.

5) Businesses managed from a plan rather than by reaction to events are more successful.

6) The completed workbook will help you communicate the direction of your business to employees, thus pointing everyone in the same direction.

7) The process of completing your business plan will help you identify business opportunities that might otherwise be missed.

8) Most importantly, the process will focus your attention on important questions such as:

What business am I in?
Where is my business headed?
Why is it headed there?

Importance of Planning

Isn't planning just for the big companies?

Planning is appropriate for any organization that wants to approach the future with a plan of action. The future comes whether you are prepared for it or not. A business plan helps you anticipate the future and make well-informed decisions because you have thought about the alternatives you will be facing.

Is planning really an important management function?

There are five functions of business management:

Plan
Organize
Staff
Direct
Control

Planning is the first of the five and establishes the basis needed to do the other functions successfully.

Can't I hire someone to do this for me?

No! This is your business we are talking about. If the business plan is to be useful, it must reflect your ideas and efforts—not those of an outsider. If you feel more comfortable obtaining outside assistance, use that help to review what you have done and make suggestions. But you must make the initial attempt at developing your plan.

Why is planning so important?

The process of planning forces you to look at the future operations of your business and anticipate what will happen. This process better prepares you for the future and makes you more knowledgeable about your business. You can analyze the past, react to the present, and plan for the future.

Importance of Planning

What role does planning play in managing a company?

Planning is a continuous process in business management. The planning process can be thought of as the six steps shown below:

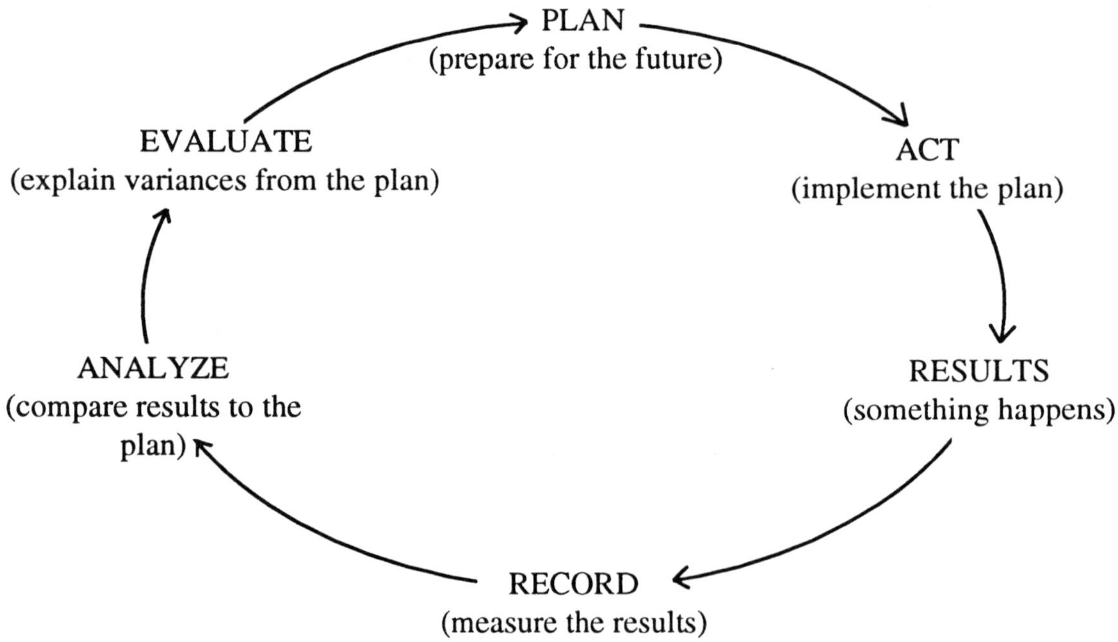

Every business is involved in the activities of making decisions and recording the results of business activities. Without a plan there is no meaningful way to analyze and evaluate the results, thus future actions are not based on a revised plan but rather revised instinct. The continual use of the planning process enables you to manage your business based on facts. Operating without a plan breaks the continuous process shown above and as a result you manage by reacting to unplanned events rather than by anticipating and planning for events. The planning process provides continual feedback to management and results in improved management decision making.

How can I possibly know the answers to all these questions?

You are not expected to know all the answers. Planning is done most successfully when the business owner involves other people in the process. You should talk to customers, employees, suppliers, bankers, professional advisors, and other business owners. Planning works best when done on a decentralized rather than centralized basis.

Importance of Planning

Am I merely putting in writing how the business operates?

No! Your present operating methods provide a starting point, but all parts of your plan should be looked at from the point of view of a beginner. You will benefit the most if you can open your mind to a wide variety of new business options. Try to avoid either-or thinking and look at the whole range of choices that are available. Be creative and innovative!

How often do I have to do this?

Continuously! A plan must be revised as needed, at least once a year. As previously discussed, planning is a continuous process. You will be surprised how much easier the plan is after the first time, and, after a revision or two, just how much you know about your business.

What's the bottom line for me if I do the plan?

Studies show that failure rates for businesses that use a business plan as a management tool are significantly lower than for businesses without a plan.

Your Mission Statement

Every business must have an ultimate purpose, a "Mission." The Mission Statement is one of the most important parts of your business plan. It expresses both your vision and your philosophy of doing business.

Step 1: Define the purpose of your business plan.

Your first decision is to clearly understand and define the purpose of your business and the reason for writing this business plan. Your purpose may be to obtain financing, create a guide for managing your business, clarify your business operation, or some combination of factors. Answer the following questions.

A) Who will use your business plan?
B) What do you hope to accomplish by writing this plan?

Step 2: Create a mission statement.

A mission statement reflects the *core* purpose of your business. The mission statement should reflect the highest goals of the organization. It should embody the basic values of the business and its employees. The mission statement must be short and focused (no more than 20 words). It should be stated in the present tense, in positive terms, and without "qualifiers." Write a one-sentence mission statement about your business. If you need to, write a longer statement and cut it down to size by going back and removing the adjectives, adverbs, and words between commas.

Step 3: Create a marketing slogan.

A marketing slogan is a short, clever, and often humorous translation of your mission statement. It is meant to convey a single, simple thought about your business that is useful to your customers. It you were writing a commercial, it would be the short sentence that comes after your company name.

Your Mission Statement

Step 1: Define the purposes of your business plan:

Step 2: Create a mission statement:

Step 3: Create a marketing slogan:

Goals and Objectives

Planning terminology can be very confusing and the terms are often used inconsistently. In this section you will be dealing with setting goals and objectives for your business.

Goals are targets for your business that are three to five years into the future. Each goal must be stated in a quantitative manner that allows you to track progress towards the goal. In other words, every goal must be measurable. Each goal should be identified with a function of the business but not an individual. Some goals may be applicable to the entire company, but some function should be made responsible for meeting the goal. It is important that all goals are compatible with the mission statement and with each other.

Objectives are targets for your business that you hope to achieve in the next year. Like goals, every objective must be measurable. Every objective should be an assigned responsibility of some individual within your business. All objectives should relate to at least one goal that you have established.

When setting goals and objectives ask the following questions:

A) What?
B) Why?
C) How?
D) When?
E) Who?

Goals and objectives can be set for any aspect of your business, but targets are commonly set for the following:

A) Sales volume
B) Profit
C) Customer satisfaction
D) Owner compensation
E) Number of employees
F) Owner time commitment
G) Assets

Step 1: Set goals.

Step 2: Set objectives.

Goals and Objectives

Goals:

Objectives:

Sources of Information

Basing your business plan and decisions on facts rather than personal beliefs is important to the success of your business. There are many sources of information about your particular type of business available. Use this information often.

Step 1: Identify appropriate trade associations.

Encyclopedia of Associations
Gale Research Company; Detroit, MI
Annual Directory

National Trade and Professional Associations
Columbia Books Inc.; Washington, DC
Annual Directory

Step 2: Identify available industry publications.

Most industries have publications with valuable information about managing a business in that industry. Consult with your trade associations, suppliers, and your local librarian who can help you identify available publications.

Step 3: Identify federal government publications.

The U.S. government is a valuable source of free and low-cost information. Check with your local librarian or call the U.S. government information number listed in your phone book.

U.S. Industrial Outlook
U.S. Department of Commerce
Annual Edition

Business Statistics
Dept. of Commerce—Bureau of Economic Analysis
Annual Edition

State and Metropolitan Area Data Book
Dept. of Commerce—Bureau of Census
Annual Edition

Statistical Abstract of the United States
Dept. of Commerce—Bureau of Census
Annual Edition

County and City Data Book
Dept. of Commerce—Bureau of Census
Annual Edition

Step 4: Identify other sources of business information.

There are many general business magazines and books that you may want to read. Ask your local Small Business Development Center counselor or other local business owners for ideas.

Small Business Sourcebook
Gale Research Company; Detroit, MI
7th Edition, November 1993

Annual Statement Studies
Robert Morris Associates; Philadelphia, PA
Annual Edition

Thomas Register of American Manufacturers and Catalog File
Thomas Publishing Company; New York, NY
Annual Directory

Sources of Information

Trade associations:

Industry publications:

Government publications:

Other general business publications:

Key Contacts

An important factor in the success of your business is your ability to solve problems through other people. In this section you will list the people that can be valuable resources for your business.

Step 1: Who is the Director of your Chamber of Commerce?

The local Chamber of Commerce is a good place to meet other business owners, get to know the director.

Step 2: Who is your trade association contact person?

Your trade association is familiar with the various challenges of your business. Find out who in the trade association is available to help you.

Step 3: Meet your local librarian.

Small business owners tend to ignore their local librarian as a valuable contact person. In a metropolitan area your library may even have a business librarian. Meet your librarian and learn what assistance is available.

Step 4: Meet your local SBDC Director.

Your local Small Business Development Center continually provides counseling to a wide variety of business owners. The counselors are people with business education and experience. They can assist you with your business plan.

Step 5: Identify other local business and civic organizations.

For many types of businesses being active in local organizations is a key to success. Determine which organizations would be of benefit to you and your business.

Step 6: Identify representatives of suppliers.

Many owners think of suppliers as merely the person that sells them products. Oftentimes these representatives have considerable knowledge of the industry. Get to know more about these people and their backgrounds.

Key Contacts

Chamber of Commerce Director:

Trade Association contact person:

Local business librarian:

Small Business Development Center Director:

Local business and civic organizations:

Representatives of suppliers:

Background

Step 1: Describe the background of your industry.

A) How has the industry developed?
B) What has been the industry's growth patterns?
C) What is the industry's future?
D) How does international trade impact the industry?
E) How well do small businesses prosper in the industry?
F) How are small businesses affected by large companies?
G) How are small businesses affected by franchises?
H) How does your business fit into the industry?

Step 2: Document assumptions about the industry.

Refer to the U.S. Industrial Outlook. Include assumption about trends in the industry (stable, growing, declining); your particular market niche (stable, growing, declining); expected impact of changes in technology.

Step 3: Describe background of your existing business.

If you are in the process of starting a new business, this step does not apply. However, if you are already in business or are considering purchasing an existing business, then answering the following questions could prove valuable.

A) When was your business founded?
B) Why was your business started?
C) Who started the business?
D) Why has the business been successful?
E) What have been key points of business growth?
F) What have been the profitability patterns?
G) How has the business purpose changed over time?

Background

Background of your industry:

Industry assumptions:

History of the business:

Timetable

This is a work sheet that you will need to update on a regular basis. The purpose is to assure that key activities vital to the future success of your business are identified and completed.

Step 1: Identify key activities.

Review all sections of your business plan, compile a list of key activities that are vital to the successful operation of your business.

Step 2: Assign responsibility for each activity.

For each identified activity, assign one person primary responsibility for the completion of that activity.

Step 3: Determine scheduled start date.

For each activity, determine the date when work will begin. You should consider how the activity fits into your overall plan as well as the availability of the person responsible.

Step 4: Determine scheduled finish date.

For each activity determine when the activity must be completed. Be realistic—a person outside of your organization may judge your managerial ability based on your ability to meet these deadlines.

Timetable

Activity	Person	Start Date	Finish Date

Products/Services - Description

Products fall into two basic categories - Industrial and Consumer.

Industrial Products - are those things used to create other goods, or in servicing the production of goods and services.

Consumer Products - are those things purchased by the intended end user.

For the purpose of this workbook, the term "product" can include both products and services.

Step 1: Specify what you intend to sell.

Copy the worksheet at the right for each product or service you sell. Write in the product's or service's name.

Step 2: Describe the product.

What does it do?
Why should people buy it?
What makes it unique or special?
How expensive or difficult is it to make?
How much will you sell it for?

Step 3: Repeat these steps for each product you sell.

Compare the individual product descriptions. Some may have several characteristics in common and could be grouped into "families" of products, or product "lines."

Step 4: Review for compatibility.

Does this product fit into the overall mission of your business? Does it compliment the other products you sell? It is important that each product blend smoothly into your overall business concept.

Products/Services - Description

Step 1: Specify what you intend to sell.

Step 2: Describe the product.

Price/Quality Relationship

Consumers consistently evaluate retail products by some combination of price and quality. Of course there are other conscious and unconscious factors which can govern behavior, but price and quality are the two factors commonly found in nearly all purchase decisions.

Each product has a product identity, or profile, based on the balance of these two variables. Competition *begins* by evaluating the perceived differences in each product's basic price/quality profile. Product profiles tend to run in cycles based on product age. Examples of the four basic profile combinations are:

Low Price/High Quality – An ideal product profile which balances price and quality in the customer's favor. Many new businesses establish themselves with this profile because it competes so easily with the other three possible profiles.

High Price/High Quality – As demand for a product increases, producers realize they can increase the price assuming quality also remains high. Mercedes Benz, Curtis Mathes Television, Rolex, and Nikon are all representative of this group.

High Price/Low Quality – Companies with older well-established products are lured by the profit inherent in cheapening the product and coasting on a quality reputation. Customers, once betrayed, seldom give these products a second chance.

Low Price/Low Quality – The "discount" philosophy of many mass merchandisers was once thought to be the wave of the future. Because product quality from discounter to discounter is the same, price assumes greater significance.

Step 1: Describe the relationship between price and quality in your product.

Evaluate the price and quality of your major products and the perceived price/quality of your business as a whole. Mark the product position on the circle with an *x*. Now place a *y* on the circle in the position where your overall company profile fits.

Step 2: Identify your competitors' product profiles.

Identify four major competitors and write their names in the indicated spaces. Note each one's overall profile on the cycle chart with a 1, 2, 3 or 4.

You may want to skip this part until you have completed the section on competition in order to evaluate your competitors' overall business profiles. You can then return and complete this step.

Price/Quality Relationship

Step 1: Describe the relationship between price and quality in your product.

Defining Your Price/Quality Relationship

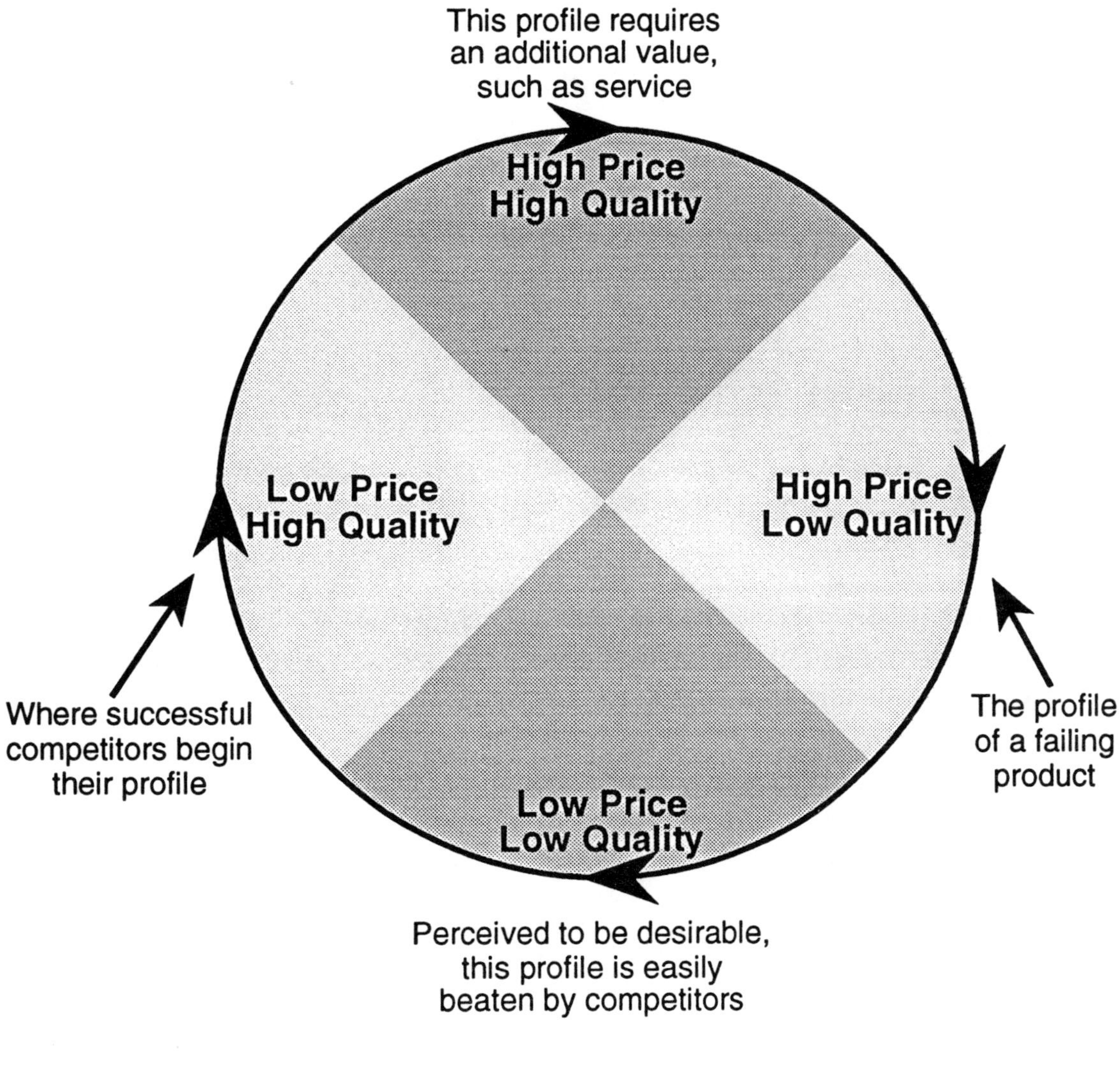

Step 2: Identify your competitors' product profiles.

Competitor #1 ____

Competitor #2 ____

Competitor #3 ____

Competitor #4 ____

Products/Services - Life Cycles

Every product has a lifespan, and your promotional priorities are also influenced by that product's place in its life-cycle. For example, promoting for an established product is generally different from that of a new one. Pricing considerations for a declining product are considerably different than those for a growing one. Competition among new products is often keener than among established ones.

Step 1: Copy the following worksheet for each product you sell.

Step 2: Assign each product a place in the product life-cycle.

Some of the factors influencing a product's position in the product life-cycle include how long it's been around, visibility, familiarity to users, frequency of use, and popularity over alternative products. Length of existence is not always a reliable way of gauging a products life cycle. Campbell Soup has been around over a hundred years, yet it is still only in its maturity. Disco boots completed their life cycle in less than three years.

Step 3: Understanding your product's "season."

Get your gross sales figures for the previous year. If this is a new business, you will need to project your gross sales. Divide that figure by 12 to arrive at a monthly average. Your monthly average is the same as the Avg. line of this chart. Now examine the actual sales you made in each month of the last year. Place a dot in the appropriate monthly column to show how much your actual monthly sales differed from the average. Now connect the dots to see your product's buying season. You can estimate this chart or use the formula on the next page to calculate an actual percent increase or decline.

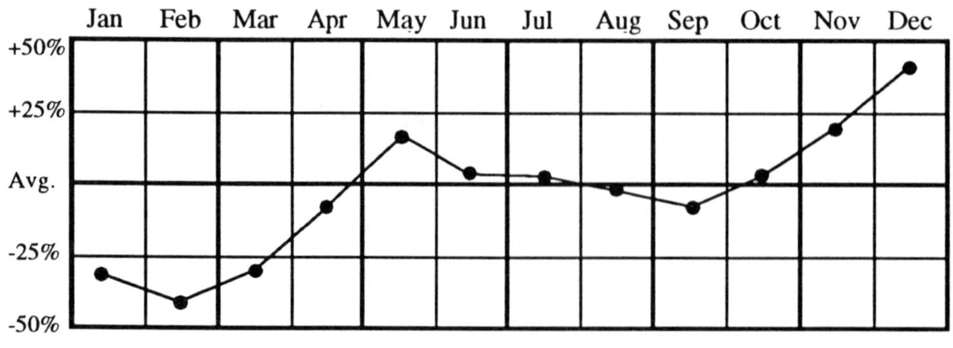

Products/Services - Life Cycles

Step 1: Product Identity

PRODUCT ____

Step 2: Position on the product life-cycle

1( ) New Product (first sales)

2( ) Growing Purchase (rapid increase)

3( ) Established Position (sales peak)

4( ) Maturity (sales hold steady)

5( ) Loss of Value (sales fall off)

6( ) Declining Purchase (rapid loss of sales)

Step 3: Chart you product's seasonality

Product Buying Cycle

	Jan	Feb	Mar	Apr	May	Jun	Jul	Aug	Sep	Oct	Nov	Dec
+50%												
+25%												
Avg.												
-25%												
-50%												

How to Calculate Percent Differences

Always divide the first number by the second number. In this case the second number is the *average*. To convert the resulting decimal to a percent: If the first number is *larger*, subtract 1 from the result, then move the decimal point two places to the right. If the first number is *smaller*, subtract the result from 1 then move the decimal point two places to the right and put a minus sign in front of it. The example below shows both methods.

Where first number is *larger*	\$650 ÷ \$500 = 1.30 (subtract 1 from result and move the decimal two places to the right) = +30%
Where first number is *smaller*	\$350 ÷ \$500 = .70 (subtract result from 1, move decimal two places to the right, add a minus) = -30%

Customers

Your customers are the most important part of your business. Without customers you wouldn't be in business. It's critical to carefully analyze who your customers are, how much and how often they buy from you, and why they do business with you rather than someone else.

Defining Customers

Marketers usually define their customers by their physical characteristics such as age, gender, occupation, income, etc. These are important because they represent the natural categories of customers. Some of the more common customer characteristics include:

Gender - Men and women exhibit very different habits when it comes to purchasing.
Age - is second only to gender as most important characteristic to measure.
Income - is a good indicator because it often shows whether the customer can buy.
Occupation - relates closely with age, income, and education.
Location - can be designated in any of several different ways.
Family status - Couples needs differ significantly from singles.
Children - Households with children can exhibit very different buying habits.
Education - is an indicator of advertising comprehension, reasoning power, etc.
Ethnic origin - People from different cultures have different values and needs.

Step 1: Identify your customers' characteristics.

Examine the list of Customer Characteristics on the worksheet. Choose the three or four that you use most often to identify or define your customers. If you plan to purchase advertising space in a mass media such as newspapers, radio, or television, you should probably include gender and age as characteristics.

Step 2: Describe your customers' most common characteristics.

For each of the characteristics you selected in Step 1, think about the way this group should be further broken down for measurement purposes. Age, for example, is usually broken down by those less than 18, those 18 to 24, those 25 to 34, those 35 to 49, those 50 to 64, and those over 65. Gender is simply men and women.

Space has been provided for you to break down your four top customer characteristics. List the one you consider to be most important first, the second most important second, and so forth. Under each characteristic, describe the *part* of that group which most often buys from you. Be as precise as you can.

Customers

Step 1: Identify your customers' characteristics.

Customer Characteristics

☐ Gender	☐ Age	☐ Income	☐ Occupation
☐ Location	☐ Marital Status	☐ Children	☐ Education
☐ Race	☐ Religion	☐ Ethnic Origin	☐ Home Ownership
☐ Job Title	☐ Industry Type	☐ Experience	☐ Previous Purchase
☐ Authority	☐ Annual Sales	☐ Orientation	☐ Interests

☐ Other ____________________

Step 2: Describe your customers' most common characteristics.

Customer Group # __________

Characteristic ____________________

____

____

____

____

Characteristic ____________________

____

____

____

____

Characteristic ____________________

____

____

____

____

Characteristic ____________________

____

____

____

____

Marketing Research

Marketing research can help you learn many things about your business. One of the most important is an idea of how many customers you potentially have, and how many of these potential customers are likely to become actual buyers.

The information you need to identify and count potential customers falls into four basic areas: **a**. information within your own files, **b**. information available to everyone (known as secondary sources), **c**. research you do yourself, and **d**. research you pay to have done.

Step 1: Determine the number of your potential customers.

This step requires doing homework. If you are selling to the general public, you need to look at the US Census data for your market area. Census information is usually available in the reference section of your local library. If you sell to other businesses, there are many potential sources of information; one of the best is a trade association. Check with your local SBDC office or visit the reference section of the library. Once you have determined the total number of potential customers living within your geographical area, write the number in the space on the worksheet.

Step 2: Determine the number that will likely purchase from you.

This is a very tough question! You need to consider your competition, both in numbers and quality. We will address the influence of competition on your business in the next section. You also need to realize that some potential customers will not buy the product from either you or your competitors.

Step 3: Determine your average customer sales per year.

This step requires doing more homework. Trade association or industry publications are good sources of information needed to answer these questions.

Step 4: Determine your annual sales volume.

You now know the number of customers and the average amount each customer will spend per year. Multiply these two numbers together to calculate your expected annual sales volume.

Step 5: Evaluate the annual sales volume figure.

Does the number you calculated in the previous step make sense? If not, go back to the first step and try again. What *assumptions* have you made about your customers? How accurate or risky are these assumptions? You want to substitute actual figures derived from some information source for your assumptions whenever possible.

Marketing Research

Step 1: Determine the number of your potential customers.

Total number of potential customers. ____________________

Step 2: Determine the number that will likely purchase from you.

A. Total annual sales volume for your product or service. ________________________

B. Number of customers who will purchase from you or one of your competitors. _________

C. Percentage of those making a purchase who will buy from you. ________%

D. Multiply the number in B by the percent in C to determine the number of potential customers that will purchase from your business. ___________________

E. Justify your calculations. Why do you believe these numbers are accurate?

____

Step 3: Determine your average customer sales per year.

A. How many purchases will your average customer make in a year? _________________

B. How much will they spend on each purchase? $_______________
(This may be for one product or a group of products typically bought together)

C. Multiply A * B to determine the annual spending of an average customer.
$__________________

Step 4: Determine your annual sales volume.

Multiply 2(D) * 3(C) $_____________________

Competitive Analysis

A key to the success of your business is establishing a unique market niche. In this section you will compare your business to your three major competitors. Use the form on the following page to record the rankings. Be honest with yourself—the purpose is to help identify areas where you have a competitive advantage as well as areas for potential improvement.

Use the worksheet at right to analyze your competitive position in relationship to three of your competitors. Remember, be honest with yourself.

Step 1: Identify your three major competitors.

List names and addresses of your three most significant competitors. Significance can be a matter of sales volume, geographic location, similarity of products, or similarity of business practices.

Step 2: Compare your business to the competition.

For each area below, rank your own business and each of your competitors on a scale of 1 to 5, with 1 being lowest and 5 highest. More than one business can have the same ranking if they are equal in that area.

1. **Products** - Which products do the better job?
2. **Price** - Consistency is generally the best plan.
3. **Quality** - How long does it last, how good is the workmanship?
4. **Product selection** - How complete is the product line?
5. **Customer service** - How politely and thoroughly is service performed?
6. **Product service** - Is the product serviced correctly and quickly?
7. **Reliability** - Does the product require frequent service or repair?
8. **Expertise** - The more knowledgeable the staff, the better.
9. **Image/Reputation** - How important is the company or product name?
10. **Location** - Consider accessibility, parking, convenience, and visibility.
11. **Layout** - Is the space efficiently utilized?
12. **Appearance** - Does the appearance match the customer's expectations?
13. **Sales methods** - Is the staff polite and effective at making sales?
14. **Credit policy** - Can customers use a variety of payment methods?
15. **Availability** - Does the customer have to wait for a product to arrive?
16. **Management** - Does the store owner take an active part in the business?
17. **Longevity/Stability** - In general, older businesses are considered more stable.
18. **Advertising** - Those who advertise are more visible than those who don't.

Step 3: Prioritize the competitive factors.

Determine the relative importance of each of these competitive factors. Assign the top priority a 1, the second a 2, etc. until you have ranked all 18 by priority.

Step 4: List changes you can make to improve your competitive position.

Write down the two or three specific actions you can take to improve your competitive position. Try to focus on those areas with a high priority.

Competitive Analysis

Step 1: Identify your three major competitors:

A: ______________________________

B: ______________________________

C: ______________________________

Steps 2 & 3: Compare your business to the competition and prioritize.

Factors	You	Competitor A	Competitor B	Competitor C	Priority
1. Products	____	____	____	____	____
2. Price	____	____	____	____	____
3. Quality	____	____	____	____	____
4. Product selection	____	____	____	____	____
5. Customer service	____	____	____	____	____
6. Product service	____	____	____	____	____
7. Reliability	____	____	____	____	____
8. Expertise	____	____	____	____	____
9. Image/Reputation	____	____	____	____	____
10. Location	____	____	____	____	____
11. Layout	____	____	____	____	____
12. Appearance	____	____	____	____	____
13. Sales methods	____	____	____	____	____
14. Credit policy	____	____	____	____	____
15. Availability	____	____	____	____	____
16. Management	____	____	____	____	____
17. Longevity/Stability	____	____	____	____	____
18. Advertising	____	____	____	____	____

Step 4: List changes you can make to improve your competitive position:

____

____

____

Marketing Strategy

Good planning can save you time and money when you put your ad campaigns together. It will be a valuable tool when you are working with your selected advertising mediums.

You can use one of three basic types of marketing strategies:

Targeted marketing strategy - which reflects a base of customers that is unique, very well defined, concentrated in a particular area, or limited in some way.
General marketing strategy - reflects a customer base which includes a wide variety of people, a large market area, or a large number of buyers.
Combination marketing strategy - which reflects a blend of both targeted customers and general customers.

Step 1: Name the product or service.

Make a copy of this worksheet for each product you sell. Also complete a worksheet for your overall business.

Step 2: Describe your strategy definers.

Answer the questions about your product or business by checking the appropriate box.

Step 3: Identify your strategy focus.

Add together the numbers next to the boxes you checked in Step 2. If the total is between 12 and 19, you strategy should focus on targeted methods of marketing. If the total is between 20 and 28, you need a more generalized marketing strategy. Totals of 29 or more indicate the need for a combination strategy of both targeted and generalized marketing. The list under each category in this step gives examples of methods which can be used effectively with that type of strategy.

Marketing Strategy

Step 1: Name the product or service.

Product: ____

Step 2: Describe your strategy definers.

I have several other competitors in town.	1☐ Yes	2☐ No	3☐ Somewhat
My customers live relatively close by.	1☐ Yes	2☐ No	3☐ Somewhat
My customers are pretty similar in nature.	1☐ Yes	2☐ No	3☐ Somewhat
My product has a specialized use.	1☐ Yes	2☐ No	3☐ Somewhat
People hear about me from other people.	1☐ Yes	2☐ No	3☐ Somewhat
I do a lot of repeat business.	1☐ Yes	2☐ No	3☐ Somewhat
Only certain people can use my product.	1☐ Yes	2☐ No	3☐ Somewhat
My advertising doesn't work that well.	1☐ Yes	2☐ No	3☐ Somewhat
I do most of my business in town.	1☐ Yes	2☐ No	3☐ Somewhat
My product isn't purchased impulsively.	1☐ Yes	2☐ No	3☐ Somewhat
People don't travel very far to visit me.	1☐ Yes	2☐ No	3☐ Somewhat
My customers tend to be unique.	1☐ Yes	2☐ No	3☐ Somewhat

Step 3: Identify your strategy focus.

Total from Step 2.____________ (Check the box below which matches this total)

12 to 19	20 to 28	29 to 36
☐ Targeted	☐ Generalized	☐ Combination
Mailings based on definers	*Newspapers*	*Specific newspaper sections*
Door-to-door contacts	*Network television*	*Radio*
In-store displays	*News magazines*	*Cable televison*
Organziation memberships	*Bus signs*	*Billboards*
Customer mailings	*Mass mailings*	*Specialty advertising*
Referrals	*News stories*	*Special interest magazines*
Word-of-mouth		*Sponsorships*
Industry publications		*Posters/banners*
Personal correspondence		*Items from columns 1&2 as needed*

Advertising Budget

The two most valuable resources you have to invest are money and time. If you don't have a lot of money to spend on advertising, you can devote additional time in public relations or sales. Five ways to calculate the amount to spend on marketing include:

A percentage of annual sales
A list of specific marketing activities
Matching your competitors advertising
Buying advertising as you go
Spending whatever is "left over" on marketing.

A good simple budget can be prepared by blending the percentage, activity, and matching forms of budgeting.

Step 1: Develop a percentage advertising budget.

Insert your projected total income for the next year from the sales forecast section of this workbook. Decide on the percent you wish to devote to marketing. For most people this can be anything from 2 percent to 15 percent. If you are new in business, you can contact your trade association for help in projecting both income and the percent generally dedicated to advertising within your industry. A new business will probably require a higher percent than an established one.

Step 2: Identify your major promotional event/focus for each month.

Make a list of the promotional activities you want to accomplish in each quarter of the coming year. You can get estimated costs for these activities from the people who perform them. Add together the costs in each quarter to arrive at a quarterly total, then add the quarterly amounts together to arrive at an annual budget.

Step 3: Develop a competitive matching advertising budget.

You can't estimate how much your competitors are spending unless you know what they are doing. Do some homework. Visit their businesses, collect samples of their advertising and get estimates from advertising professionals on the cost to produce a similar advertising campaign.

Step 4: Formulate a comprehensive advertising budget.

Write in the annual amounts you calculated in each step above. Now average them and write the average in the space provided. This is a good estimate of what you should be spending on advertising. Make any final up or down adjustments based on your own judgement before writing a Final Annual Budget figure at the end of the worksheet.

Now divide the total marketing budget into monthly amounts. Use the Product Life Cycle chart completed earlier in this workbook to guide you in allocating money to each month.

Advertising Budget

Step 1: Percentage advertising budget.

a. Projected gross annual income $__________

b. Percent to be allocated for advertising. ________ %

Percentage-based marketing budget (a x b) $__________

Step 2: Activity advertising budget.

Cost of tasks planned in first quarter $__________

Cost of tasks planned in second quarter $__________

Cost of tasks planned in third quarter $__________

Cost of tasks planned in fourth quarter $__________

Total of tasks planned for the year $__________

Step 3: Competitive matching advertising budget.

Amount spent by your major competitor in:

Radio	$________	Direct mail	$________
TV	$________	Stationary	$________
Newspaper	$________	Packaging	$________
Magazines	$________	Displays	$________
Billboards	$________	Brochures	$________
Catalogs	$________	Other	$________

Total spent by competitor in a year $__________

Step 4: Comprehensive advertising budget.

a. Percentage budget $__________

b. Task budget $__________

c. Competitive budget $__________

Average budget amount (a+b+c÷3) $__________

Final Annual Budget (adjusted average budget) $__________

(Divide the Final annual Budget into 12 monthly allocations)

Location

Step 1: Describe the location of your business.

A) What is the address of your business?
B) What features make this a good location for your business?
C) What nearby businesses will help you attract customers?

Step 2: Describe the appearance of your business.

A) What are the physical features of your building?
B) What are the appearances of other nearby businesses?

Step 3: Determine future needs of your location.

A) What renovations will be needed and what are the costs?
B) What are the prospects for business growth in the area?

Step 4: Prepare visual aids to show location to outsiders.

Location is an extremely important factor for any business. For most retail and many small service businesses, location can be critical to success. For retail and service businesses, customer access is extremely important when evaluating a location. For wholesale and manufacturing businesses, the availability of resources—such as labor, materials, transportation, and utilities—are very important. It is often easier to describe your location to an outsider through use of maps, pictures, and a diagram of the layout.

A) Take pictures of your business and the surrounding businesses in your area.

B) On a copy of a map of the area, indicate the location of your business and any major reference points.

C) Draw an accurate diagram of your floor space, indicating location of equipment, furniture, and fixtures.

Step 5: Identify occupancy costs of location.

Go to page 38

Location

Location of business: ______

______

______

______

______

Appearance of business: ______

______

______

______

______

Future needs of the location: ______

______

______

______

______

Visual aids checklist

Pictures: ______
Map: ______
Floorspace diagram: ______
Other: ______

______

______

______

______

______

Occupancy Expenses

There are many costs of maintaining a business location in addition to the basic monthly rent. This section requires you to identify all of these costs on a monthly basis. Many costs vary greatly by month and have an impact on your cash flow.

Step 1:

Check the expenses that are applicable to your business location.

Step 2:

Fill in the monthly costs for all applicable cost categories.

Step 3:

Calculate the monthly totals—add down the columns.

Step 4:

Calculate the annual totals for each expenses category—add across the rows.

Step 5:

Check for accuracy—column totals and row totals should match.

Occupancy Expenses

	1	2	3	4	5	6	7	8	9	10	11	12	Yearly Total
Rent/mortgage payments													
Property taxes													
Maintenance/repairs													
Insurance													
Electric													
Gas													
Water/Sewer													
Telephone (base charge)													
Garbage													
Other													
TOTALS													

Forms of Doing Business

There are five primary forms of doing business that may be appropriate for your small business. The five forms are described briefly below. You should seek competent tax and legal advice to complete the steps.

Sole Proprietorship:

Your business is completely owned and operated by you. You own all assets and are entitled to all profits that may be produced, but you also are responsible for all liabilities and must suffer the consequences of all losses that may result. It is extremely easy to start this type of business and there are no taxes other than your individual income taxes.

General Partnership:

Your business is owned and operated by you and at least one other person. Together you share profits and losses and the assets and liabilities according to a written partnership agreement (which is recommended but not required). You and your partners have legal liability for one another's acts. Partners pay income taxes on their individual shares of the profits, but not tax on the partnership.

Limited Partnership:

This form of doing business is similar to a general partnership, but there are two types of partners—general and limited. Limited partners are limited in legal liability to an amount based on their capital contribution to the business.

Regular Corporation:

A corporation is a separate legal entity formed by you alone or in conjunction with other owners. A corporation must have articles of incorporation and bylaws. You normally need a lawyer to properly establish a corporation. A corporation can do business in its own name, separate from you and the other owners. Owners are usually limited in their liability to an amount based on their investment in stock. Corporations must pay corporate income taxes and the owners must pay individual taxes on any salaries or dividends they receive from the corporation.

Chapter S Corporation:

This is a special corporation—like a regular corporation in all legal aspects—in which the owners are taxed like the owners of a partnership.

Step 1: Identify advantages and disadvantages of each form for your business.

Step 2: Determine the form of doing business you will use.

Forms of Doing Business

Advantages and disadvantages of a sole proprietorship:

Advantages and disadvantages of a general partnership:

Advantages and disadvantages of a limited partnership:

Advantages and disadvantages of a regular corporation:

Advantages and disadvantages of an S corporation:

Selected form of doing business:

Management

Step 1: Identify owners and key employees.

A) What form of doing business have you selected?
B) Who are the owners and what are their titles?
C) Who are the key employees and what are their titles?
D) When have these people previously worked together?

Step 2: Develop a resume for each owner and key employee.

Each resume should contain the person's name and title and answer the following questions in order:

A) What are the most important duties?
B) What is the previous business experience?
C) What is the educational background?
D) What are the personal interests?
E) Who are the references?

Step 3: Identify outside consultants and advisors.

A) Who is your accountant? ________________________
B) Who is your lawyer? ________________________
C) Who is your banker? ________________________
D) Who is your insurance broker? ________________________
E) Who are other key outsiders? ________________________

Step 4: Complete the management skills matrix.

The purpose of this exercise is to help you identify areas of business expertise where you need to seek assistance. For each skill area, check the adequate knowledge column with an "I" to indicate that an insider (owner or key employee) has the skill or an "O" to indicate an outsider has the skill. For each skill area where you have not indicated adequate knowledge, check either the assistance needed or education needed column with an "X."

Step 5: Determine how to address needed skill areas.

For each skill area checked with an "X," determine how you will compensate where management skill is lacking.

Management

Owners and key employees:

Resumes: (Use separate page for each resume)

Outside consultants and advisors:

Management Skills Matrix	Adequate Knowledge	Assistance Needed	Education Needed
Accounting & taxes			
Planning			
Organizing			
Financial management			
People management			
Time management			
Sales			
Promotion			
Decision-making			
Cost control			
Personnel policies			
Pricing			

Plan to compensate for areas where management skill is lacking: (Attach extra pages if necessary)

Personnel

Step 1: Identify needed employees.

Written job descriptions that clearly define the duties of each employee and a written personnel policies manual that details the relationship between employee and employer are vital documents.

A) How many employees do you need to run your business?
B) List the job titles and skills needed by employees.
C) Do you have written job descriptions? If not, when will you complete written job descriptions?
D) Do you have a written personnel manual? If not, when will you complete a written personnel manual?

Step 2: Identify source of employees.

Good employees can make the difference between a successful business and a marginal one. It is important to know where to find qualified employees.

A) Where will you obtain needed employees?
B) What process will you use to screen and hire employees (e.g. job skill testing; job interviews; drug testing; etc.)?

Step 3: Specify employee training needs.

Training for new employees and retraining for existing employees is critical to operating a successful business.

A) What training is needed for new employees? Specify training needs for each position.
B) What training is needed for existing employees? Specify training needs for each position.
C) Who will conduct employee training (in-house; paid consultants; community college; etc.)?
D) Estimate the cost for employee training.

Personnel

Needed employees:

Source of employees:

Employee training:

Salaries and Wages

Salary and wage expense is your first major category of operating expenses. In this section you will calculate only the wage and salary cost of having employees working for your business. Payroll taxes required by law, and optional fringe benefits you agree to pay for your employees will be covered in the next section.

It's likely the number of employees (and hours worked) will vary from month to month, especially if your business has seasonal highs and lows. Don't forget to include the wages of part-time employees.

Step 1:

Fill in a brief title for each employee required in your business. This includes active owners and managers.

Step 2: Document assumptions about your employees.

Be sure to include an assumption regarding wage level changes. These changes may be significantly different from the inflation rate. Be sure to consider impact of changes in unemployment rates.

Inflation rate: ______ %

Unemployment rate: ______ %

Wage increases: ______ %

Step 3:

Fill in the salary or wage to be paid each employee for each month.

Step 4:

Calculate the total monthly salaries—add down the columns.

Step 5:

Calculate the yearly salaries for each position—add across the rows.

Step 6:

Check for accuracy—column totals and row totals should match.

Salaries and Wages

Salary/Wage Per Month	1	2	3	4	5	6	7	8	9	10	11	12	Yearly Total
Employees													
1													
2													
3													
4													
5													
6													
7													
8													
9													
10													
11													
12													
Total Employees													
Owners													
1													
2													
3													
4													
Total Owners													
TOTAL													

Payroll Taxes and Benefits

In the previous section you budgeted for salaries and wages. In this section you will budget for both mandatory employee benefits and optional employee benefits. You may want to get some help from your accountant and your insurance agent in order to complete this section.

Step 1: Budget for mandatory employee benefits.

Mandatory benefits include:

- Social security
- Federal unemployment taxes
- State unemployment taxes
- Workers compensation insurance/state industrial accident insurance

Step 2: Budget for optional employee benefits.

Optional benefits include:

- Medical insurance
- Dental insurance
- Vision insurance
- Life insurance
- Disability insurance
- Pension plan
- Profit-sharing plan

Step 3: Calculate grand total of mandatory and optional benefits.

Step 4: Calculate benefits as a percentage of salaries and wages.

Step 5: Review benefits being offered.

Compare the type and cost of benefits you offer to industry averages and particularly to your local competition. Determine if you need to make some changes. Optional benefits can make the difference between keeping or losing a key employee.

Payroll Taxes and Benefits

Mandatory:	1	2	3	4	5	6	7	8	9	10	11	12	Yearly Total
Social Security													
Federal Unemployment													
State Unemployment													
Workers Compensation													
Other													
Total Mandatory													
Optional:													
Medical Insurance													
Dental Insurance													
Vision Insurance													
Life Insurance													
Disability Insurance													
Pension Plan													
Profit-sharing Plan													
Other													
Total Optional													
GRAND TOTALS													
% of Salaries and Wages													

Outside Services

You can obtain expertise that your company lacks by using outsiders on a contractual basis. Almost all businesses make some use of attorneys and accountants. You can also obtain expertise such as marketing and engineering on a contractual basis. You should also consider contracting for more routine services such as secretarial, equipment and building maintenance, and janitorial services.

Step 1: Determine which outside services you will be utilizing.

Review the services listed on the opposite page. Decide which services you will use in the next year. Also decide how much you will be using each service.

Step 2: Complete budget amounts for each month.

For each category of service you have selected, budget an appropriate amount for each month. For services that you have not used in the past you should obtain two or three bids to assist you with the budgeting process.

Step 3:

Calculate total expenses for each month—add down the columns.

Step 4:

Calculate yearly totals for each service—add across the rows.

Step 5:

Check for accuracy—column totals should equal row totals.

Outside Services

	1	2	3	4	5	6	7	8	9	10	11	12	Yearly Total
Accounting													
Legal													
Marketing													
Engineering													
Secretarial													
Maintenance													
Janitorial													
Other													
Totals													

Insurance

You should review your insurance needs and the adequacy of your existing policies each year with your insurance agent. A good time to do that is during the process of updating your business plan.

Step 1: Determine needed insurance coverage for next year.

Step 2: Obtain bids where appropriate.

Step 3: Investigate premium payment options.

Step 4: Complete insurance expense budget.

Insurance

	1	2	3	4	5	6	7	8	9	10	11	12	Yearly Total
Fire													
Liability													
Automobile													
Business Interruption													
Crime													
Rent													
Key Personnel													
Bonding													
Other													
TOTALS													

Debt

This debt schedule includes all debt. Whether the source is an owner, family member, relative, friend, bank, supplier, or other, the debt belongs on this schedule. This is for existing debt, not anticipated debt.

Step 1: List all debt obligations.

Each debt obligation should be listed under both principal payments and interest payments.

Step 2: Complete principal and interest payment amounts.

For each debt obligation complete the monthly principal and interest payments. This schedule should reflect when the payments are actually scheduled, do not merely put an equal amount in each month if this is not correct. Do these figures involve an assumption about future interest rates? Is it a good assumption?

Step 3:

Calculate total principal payments, total interest payments and a grand total for each month—add down the columns.

Step 4:

Calculate yearly totals for both principal and interest payments for each debt obligation.

Step 5:

Check for accuracy—column totals should equal row totals.

Debt

	1	2	3	4	5	6	7	8	9	10	11	12	Yearly Total
Principal Payments: (list source of debt)													
1) ______													
2) ______													
3) ______													
4) ______													
5) ______													
Total Principal													
Interest Payments: (list source of debt)													
1) ______													
2) ______													
3) ______													
4) ______													
5) ______													
Total Interest													
TOTALS													

Fixed Assets

This section will help you plan purchases of fixed assets. Fixed assets are defined as assets which have useful lives of more than one year. Examples include land, buildings, leasehold improvements, machines, equipment, office furniture, and computers.

This section also will help you calculate the monthly depreciation for each fixed asset. Depreciation is defined as the original cost of the equipment divided by the useful life (in months) of the equipment. For example, a truck might cost $6,000 and have a useful life of five years (60 months). The truck's monthly depreciation would be $100 per month ($6,000 divided by 60 months). This example is called "straight-line" depreciation. There are several methods for calculating depreciation. Consult with your accountant to determine the depreciation schedule most applicable to your business. Land is not depreciated.

Step 1:

List each fixed asset to be purchased during the next year.

Step 2:

Fill in the cost required to buy each fixed asset (new or used) and estimated acquisition date.

Step 3:

Estimate the useful life (in months) of each fixed asset to be purchased.

Step 4:

Fill in the monthly depreciation for each fixed asset (cost divided by the useful life in months) to be purchased.

Step 5:

Calculate the totals for fixed assets to be purchased and monthly depreciation.

Step 6:

Fill in the cost and monthly depreciation of existing fixed assets.

Step 7:

Calculate total monthly depreciation.

Fixed Assets

Fixed Assets	Cost	Acquisition Date	Useful Life (in Months)	Monthly Depreciation

Total Cost—
New Fixed Assets $__________

Monthly Depreciation-
New Fixed Assets $__________

Total Cost—
Existing Fixed Assets $__________

Monthly Depreciation-
Existing Fixed Assets $__________

Total Monthly Depreciation $__________

Miscellaneous Expenses

This budget of miscellaneous expenses should include all expenses not listed on previous budget worksheets. You have already completed budgets for:

- Wages and salaries
- Payroll taxes and benefits
- Occupancy expenses
- Advertising
- Outside services
- Insurance
- Debt
- Fixed Assets

Step 1: Compile list of miscellaneous expense categories.

The worksheet on the opposite page lists some common miscellaneous expenses. You should review your chart of accounts and old financial statements to determine others that should be listed.

Step 2: Complete monthly budget amounts.

Fill in monthly budget amounts for all miscellaneous expenses.

Step 3:

Calculate total expenses for each month—add down the columns.

Step 4:

Calculate yearly totals for each expense—add across the rows.

Step 5:

Check for accuracy—column totals should equal row totals.

Miscellaneous Expenses

	1	2	3	4	5	6	7	8	9	10	11	12	Yearly Total
Bad Debt													
Car/Delivery													
Supplies													
Other:													
Totals													

Start-up Expenses

Start-up expenses are the various expenses it takes to open your doors for business. The majority of these expenses will be one-time expenditures, while others will occur every year. Examples of these expenses are listed on the next page. If you have an existing business, skip this worksheet.

Step 1:

Fill in "Total available cash" for starting your business venture.

Step 2:

Review the expenses listed on the next page. You can probably use this list for the expenses for your business. You may have some expenses which are not listed here—write them under "Other expenses."

Step 3:

Estimate your cost for each expense.

Step 4:

Calculate the total for your start-up expenses.

Step 5:

Calculate "Beginning Cash Balance" by subtracting total start-up expenses from total available cash. This amount should also be written on page 69 in month (column) 1 for beginning cash balance.

Start-up Expenses

EXPENSE		COST
Total available cash		$ ________
Purchases of **fixed assets**	$ ________	
Beginning inventory of merchandise—for retailing businesses	________	
Legal fees	________	
Accounting fees	________	
Licenses & permits	________	
Remodeling work	________	
Deposits (public utilities, etc.)	________	
Advertising (grand opening, etc.)	________	
Promotions (door prizes, etc.)	________	
Other expenses:		
________	________	
________	________	
________	________	
________	________	
________	________	
TOTAL START-UP EXPENSES		$ ________
Less: Start-up expenses:		$ ________
Beginning Cash Balance		$ ________

Sales Forecast

Forecasting sales is critical to your business from both a management and sales point of view. If you don't know how much you plan to sell in the next 12 months, you can't plan how much to spend. Remember to be realistic in your projections. Look for trends by reviewing your own records or industry figures. You should review the sections you've completed on products, customers, competitors, and budgets to assist in defining trends.

Step 1: Estimate unit sales for the next 12 months.

Estimate the number of units you expect to sell over the next 12 months. Using your product life cycle information adjust the monthly totals to reflect seasonal fluctuations. Start out conservatively. Make copies of this page if you have more than five products.

Step 2: Insert retail prices for each product.

Fill in the retail price for an individual product in the Price Per Unit space below the Units Sold. If you plan to adjust prices over the course of the year, reflect this change in the appropriate months.

Step 3: Calculate monthly product sales.

Multiply the number of units you plan to sell in one month by the retail cost per unit for that month. Insert the total sales in dollars for that month in the space indicated.

Step 4: Calculate monthly sales total.

Add all the *Total Sales* within a column and insert this figure in the space at the bottom of each column. This is the combined monthly sales forecast for all products.

Step 5: Calculate yearly sales total for each category.

Add the *Total Sales* for each product along each row and insert this figure in the column marked Yearly Total at the end of the row. This is the total yearly sales forecast for that individual product.

Step 6: Check the accuracy of your figures.

It's easy to add a number twice or skip a number when totaling a column or row. The sum of all the figures in the Yearly Total column should match the sum of all the monthly totals along the bottom of the worksheet. *The figure in the lower right corner of the spreadsheet is your total yearly income from all products sold.*

You can easily transfer a table like this one to a computer spreadsheet program (such as Lotus 1,2,3, or Microsoft Excel) and let the computer do the calculating.

Sales Forecast

	1	2	3	4	5	6	7	8	9	10	11	12	Yearly Total
Product #1													
Units Sold													
Price per Unit													
Total Sales													
Product #2													
Units Sold													
Price per Unit													
Total Sales													
Product #3													
Units Sold													
Price per Unit													
Total Sales													
Product #4													
Units Sold													
Price per Unit													
Total Sales													
Product #5													
Units Sold													
Price per Unit													
Total Sales													
Total Sales													
All Products													

Cost of Goods Sold

In the previous section you forecast the sales of each product or service by month. In this section you will calculate the cost for the products you will sell. For example, you might sell a product for $50.00 (the retail price), but your cost of this product might be $30.00 (which includes freight).

If your business sells only a service, you will not have cost of goods sold. If so, you do not need to complete this section and can go to the next section.

To complete this section, you will need to use data from the previous section (Sales Forecast).

Step 1:

Fill in the units-sold line for your five categories for each month. Refer to page 63.

Step 2:

Fill in your cost per unit for each category. You are making some assumptions here. What are they and how much risk is involved?

Step 3:

Calculate the total cost for each of the categories—units sold x cost per unit.

Step 4:

Calculate the cost of goods sold—for each month—add down the columns.

Step 5:

Calculate the yearly sales for each category—add across the rows.

Step 6:

Check for accuracy—column totals and row totals should match.

Cost of Goods Sold

	1	2	3	4	5	6	7	8	9	10	11	12	Yearly Total
Product/Service 1													
Units Sold													
Cost/Unit													
Total Cost													
Product/Service 2													
Units Sold													
Cost/Unit													
Total Cost													
Product/Service 3													
Units Sold													
Cost/Unit													
Total Cost													
Product/Service 4													
Units Sold													
Cost/Unit													
Total Cost													
Product/Service 5													
Units Sold													
Cost/Unit													
Total Cost													
Cost of Goods Sold													
All Products													

Operating Expenses

Operating expenses include a wide variety of expenses required to operate a business. Some of these expenses are fixed—they will remain constant regardless of the sales level. For example, your rent might be $500 per month—it stays fixed and does not change as sales go up or down over the months.

On the other hand, some expenses do increase and decrease as sales increase or decrease. These expenses are variable expenses. An example might be your car/delivery expense—as your sales increase, your delivery expense probably would increase.

Step 1:

Review the expenses listed on the facing page. These all refer to previously completed budget worksheets. If you have not completed all the budget worksheets, you must do so before going on in the workbook. Owners' salaries should be included for a corporation but not for a sole-proprietorship or partnership.

Step 2:

Fill in your monthly estimate for each category of expense. Remember all of these come from other worksheets.

Step 3:

Calculate total expenses for each month—add down the columns.

Step 4:

Calculate yearly totals for each expense—add across the rows.

Step 5:

Check for accuracy—column totals and row totals should match.

Operating Expenses

	1	2	3	4	5	6	7	8	9	10	11	12	Yearly Total
Non-Labor:													
Occupancy Expenses													
Outside Services													
Insurance													
Advertising													
Miscellaneous													
Total Non-Labor													
Labor:													
Salaries & Wages													
Payroll taxes & benefits													
Total Labor													

Cash Flow Projections

Cash flow projections are among the most critical financial projections you will make. You will calculate your cash receipts and the cash disbursements for each month. If the cash receipts are greater than the cash disbursements, you will have a positive cash flow. If the cash receipts are less than the cash disbursements, you will have a negative cash flow. Negative cash flows are enclosed in brackets. Here is an example: ($5218).

Step 1:

Fill in your beginning cash balance for the first month. This amount should be taken from page 61, the start-up expenses worksheet if your business plan is for a new business.

Step 2:

Fill in the various categories for Cash Receipts and total them—for the first month only. The line labeled "Collect Accounts Receivable" needs to be carefully considered. You must know the percentage of your sales that are not cash sales and how many days it normally takes to collect credit sales.

Step 3:

Fill in the various categories for Cash Disbursements and total them—for the first month only. The line labelled "Purchases (Merchandise)" requires that you know the number of days it normally takes you to pay for a purchase.

Step 4:

Calculate the Net Cash Flow for the first month (Total Cash Receipts minus Total Cash Disbursements).

Step 5:

Calculate the Ending Cash Balance for the first month—Beginning Cash Balance plus a positive Net Cash Flow (or minus a negative Net Cash Flow).

Step 6:

Fill in the Beginning Cash Balance for the second month (which is the Ending Cash Balance for the first month).

Step 7:

Repeat the first six steps for each of the twelve months—remember to complete one month at a time!

Cash Flow Projections

	1	2	3	4	5	6	7	8	9	10	11	12	Yearly Total
Beginning Cash Balance													
Cash Receipts													
Cash Sales													
Collect Accounts Receivable													
Sales of Fixed Assets													
Miscellaneous Income													
Total Cash Receipts													
Cash Disbursements													
Cash Purchases (Merchandise)													
Pay Accounts Payable													
Labor Expenses													
Owner Withdrawals													
Non-Labor Expenses													
Purchase of Fixed Assets													
Debt Payments - old													
Total Cash Disbursed													
Net Cash Flow													
New Debt													
New Owner Investment													
New Debt-Interest Paymts													
New Debt-Principal Paymts													
New Owner Withdrawals													
Adjusted Net Cash Flow													
Ending Cash Balance													

Projected Income Statement

You are now ready to assemble the data for your projected income statement. This statement will calculate your net profit or net loss (before income taxes) for each month.

Step 1:

Fill in the sales for each month. You already estimated these figures on page 63—just recopy them on the work sheet.

Step 2:

Fill in the cost of goods sold for each month. You already estimated these figures on page 65—just recopy on the work sheet.

Step 3:

Calculate the Gross Margin for each month (Sales minus Cost of Goods Sold).

Step 4:

Fill in the total of labor-related operating expenses (salaries, mandatory benefits, optional benefits). You estimated these figures on pages 47 and 49—just recopy them.

Step 5:

Fill in the total of non-labor-related operating expenses. You estimated these figures on page 67—just recopy them. Calculate the expense labeled 'interest - new'—this is interest expense associated with the new debt. Also copy the figures for depreciation and interest on existing debt.

Step 6:

Calculate yearly totals for all categories—add across the rows.

Step 7:

Calculate the Total Operating Expenses for each month—add down the columns.

Step 8:

Calculate the Net Operating Profit for each month (Gross Margin minus Total Operating Expenses). Also calculate the yearly total. Determine the amount of other gains or loses and then calculate the Net Profit or Net Loss before income taxes.

Step 9:

For a sole partnership or partnership, copy the amount of owner withdrawals (page 47).

Projected Income Statement

	1	2	3	4	5	6	7	8	9	10	11	12	Yearly Total
Sales													
Cost of Goods Sold													
Gross Margin													
Operating Expenses													
Labor Expenses													
Non-Labor Expenses													
Depreciation													
Interest - Old Debt													
Interest - New Debt													
Total Operating Expenses													
Net Operating Profit													
Other Gains/Losses													
Net Profit (or Loss) Before Income Taxes													
Owner Withdrawals (Sole proprietorships and partnerships)													

Break-Even Analysis

The break-even point is **the** level of sales at which your total sales for the time period exactly covers your cost of goods sold and operating expenses. This level of sales is called the Break-Even Point (BEP sales level).

In other words, at the BEP sales level, you will make a zero profit. If you sell **more** than the BEP sales level, you will make a net profit. If you sell **less** than the BEP sales level, you will make a net loss.

The work sheet will calculate your BEP sales level for any year of operations.

Step 1:

Fill in your Total Sales, Cost of Goods Sold, and Variable Operating Expenses. Refer to pages 67 and 71 for these figures. Your variable operating expense are those that vary in amount as your levels of sales or production change. Calculate your Gross Margin and Contribution Margin.

Step 2:

Calculate the Contribution Margin % using the formula which is given on the work sheet. The Contribution Margin % tells you what **percentage** of each dollar of sales results in Contribution Margin.

Step 3:

Fill in the Fixed Operating Expenses. Refer to page 67. Your fixed operating expenses are those that remain constant in amount as your levels of sales or production change. Common fixed expenses are rent, utilities, and insurance premiums.

Step 4:

Calculate the BEP sales level using the formula which is given. You need to reach this level of sales just to break even.

Step 5:

What does this figure mean? This figure represents the amount of sales necessary to cover your basic operating expenses. The calculation did not include loan principal payments or owner draws if your business is a sole proprietorship. It also includes no provision for profits.

Break-Even Analysis

Step 1:

Total Sales	$____________
Cost of Goods Sold	- $____________
Gross Margin	= $____________
Variable Operating Expenses	- $____________
Contribution Margin	= $____________

Step 2:

$$\text{Contribution Margin \%} = \frac{\text{Contribution Margin}}{\text{Total Sales}} = \frac{\$\ \_\_\_\_\_\_\_\_\_\_}{\$\ \_\_\_\_\_\_\_\_\_\_}$$

Contribution Margin % = 0. ___ ___ ___
(Leave the Contribution Margin % in a decimal format. The correct format is 0.347—not 34.7%).

Step 3:

Fixed Operating Expenses = $ ____________

Step 4:

$$\text{BEP Sales Level} = \frac{\text{Fixed Operating Expenses}}{\text{Contribution Margin \%}} = \frac{\$\ \_\_\_\_\_\_\_\_\_\_}{0.\ \_\_\_\ \_\_\_\ \_\_\_}$$

BEP Sales Level = $ ____________

Balance Sheet

The balance sheet can be compared to a picture of your financial condition on a particular day. This statement is a list of your assets (what you own at your cost), and your associated liabilities (what you owe). Your equity (what you are worth) in these assets is the difference between the dollar value of the assets less the associated liabilities.

You are going to prepare a balance sheet as of the end of your last fiscal year or as of the start-up date of your business. You should include all the assets and liabilities as of the appropriate date. You will also be preparing a projected balance sheet for a date one year in the future.

Step 1:

Fill in the amounts for each of the Current Assets and calculate the Total Current Assets.

Step 2:

Fill in the amounts for each of the Fixed Assets—Land, Buildings, Equipment, and Other—less accumulated depreciation and calculate Total Fixed Assets.

Step 3:

Calculate the Total Assets (Total Current Assets + Total Fixed Assets).

Step 4:

Fill in the amounts for each liability and calculate the required totals.

Step 5:

Calculate the Owner's Equity (Total Assets - Total Liabilities).

Step 6:

Fill in the amount of Total Liabilities + Owner's Equity. This amount should equal the amount for Total Assets.

Step 7:

Repeat steps 1 through 6 for the end of the year projections.

Balance Sheet

Assets	As of ________		As of ________	
Current Assets	$ ________		$ ________	
Cash	________		________	
Accounts receivable	________		________	
Inventory	________		________	
Other current assets	________		________	
Total Current Assets		$ ________		$ ________
Fixed Assets				
Land	$ ________		$ ________	
Buildings (Less Accum. Depr.)	________		________	
Equipment (Less Accum. Depr.)	________		________	
Other fixed assets (Less A.D.)	________		________	
Total Fixed Assets		$ ________		$ ________
Total Assets		$ ________		$ ________

Liabilities				
Current Liabilities				
Accounts payable	$ ________		$ ________	
Other current liabilities	________		________	
Total Current Liabilities		$ ________		$ ________
Long-term Liabilities				
Debt	$ ________		$ ________	
Other long-term liabilities	________		________	
Total Long-term Liabilities		$ ________		$ ________
Total Liabilities		$ ________		$ ________

Owner's Equity	$ ________	$ ________
Total Liabilities + Owner's Equity	$ ________	$ ________

Projected Cash Flow Statement

The Projected Cash Flow Statement you are about to prepare should result in the same amount of cash flow as the cash flow projections you prepared on page 69. The worksheet on the next page is in a different format and requires that you have already completed the balance sheet projections on page 75.

Step 1:

Complete the blanks in the first column; all figures come from either page 73 or 75 as indicated. Be sure to indicate negative amounts by placing the amount in brackets.

Step 2:

Complete the second column by adding or subtracting the amounts shown in the first column. Be especially careful to note when to add and when to subtract. Also be careful when dealing with negative amounts (in brackets).

Step 3:

Verify accuracy by comparing the change in cash figure to the Balance Sheet on page 75.

Projected Cash Flow Statement

CASH FLOW FROM OPERATIONS:

NET PROFIT BEFORE TAXES (page 71)		$ ________
PLUS:		
Depreciation Expense (page71)	$ ________	
PLUS:		
INCREASE (DECREASE) VS. PREVIOUS PERIOD IN -		
Accounts Payable (page 75)	$ ________	
Other Current Liabilities (page 75)	________	
PLUS:		
DECREASE (INCREASE) VS. PREVIOUS PERIOD IN-		
Accounts Receivable (page 75)	$ ________	
Inventory (page 75)	________	
Other Current Assets (page 75)	________	
NET CASH FLOW FROM OPERATIONS		$ ________

CASH FLOW FROM INVESTING ACTIVITIES:

DECREASE (INCREASE) VS. PREVIOUS PERIOD IN -		
Fixed Assets (page 75)	$ ________	
NET CASH FLOW FROM INVESTING ACTIVITIES		$ ________

CASH FLOW FROM FINANCING ACTIVITIES:

INCREASE (DECREASE) VS. PREVIOUS PERIOD IN -		
Debt (page 75)	$ ________	
Other Long Term Liabilities (page 75)	________	
Owner's investment (not including profit)	________	
NET CASH FLOW FROM FINANCING ACTIVITIES		$ ________
TOTAL CASH FLOWS		$ ________
Less: Owner's withdrawal (sole proprietorships and partnerships)(page 71)	$ ________	
CHANGE IN CASH		$ ________

Summary

Step 1: Verify completion of previous pages.

You should have finished all the other sections in the workbook before continuing any further.

Step 2: Identify your business plan audience.

What type of person are you intending to satisfy with this business plan? The summary should briefly address all the major issues that are important to this person. Keep in mind that this page will probably be the first read by this person. It is extremely important the summary be brief yet contain the information most important to the reader. This section should make the reader want to read the rest of your plan.

Step 3: Write a one-page summary.

You will now need to loosen up your writing hand because it is time to write no more than a page, 25 lines to be exact, summarizing all the previous work sheets you have completed.

Determine which sections are going to be most interesting to your reader. Write one to three sentences that summarize each of the important sections.

These sentences should appear in the order of the sections of your business plan. Keep in mind that the sentences must fit together to form a summary, not appear to be a group of loosely related thoughts.

You may want to have several different summaries, depending on who will read the business plan. Your banker, a potential investor, and an employee are all interested in different information.

Summary

Supporting Exhibits

Step 1: Identify desired supporting exhibits.

Using the checklist, identify documents you will use as supporting exhibits for your business plan. You should consider that the supporting exhibits needed depend on how you will be using your completed business plan.

Step 2: Collect these supporting exhibits.

Complete any documents that are not readily available and obtain copies of items that already are in existence. Use the checklist to keep track of exhibits you have gathered and ones that still need to be assembled.

Step 3: Attach appropriate supporting exhibits to your business plan.

Each time a copy of your business plan is distributed, be sure to attach the necessary supporting exhibits. As with the summary, be sure to keep the interests of your reader in mind.

Supporting Exhibits

Exhibit	Needed?	Completed?
Historical business financial statements - 3 years		
Historical business tax returns - 3 years		
Current business credit report		
Resumes of each owner		
Recent tax return of each owner		
Organizational chart		
Job descriptions		
Floor layout (showing fixed assets)		
Photos of business		
Map showing location		
Lease/rental agreements		
Loan documents		
Credit reports of major customers		
Patents		
Letters of reference		
Market survey report		

Working With Your Banker

Your newly completed business plan can be used as the foundation for a loan proposal to your local banker. This section contains some valuable information about working with your banker.

Your business plan should be attached to a one-page cover letter that summarizes your loan request. Address this cover letter to your loan officer and briefly cover the five following points:

1) Purpose of the loan
2) Amount required
3) Term of the loan
4) Source of repayment
5) Collateral available

Your loan proposal serves two primary purposes: 1) to educate your banker about your business. It is best to assume that bankers know nothing about your business and industry and that it is your job to educate them; 2) to demonstrate that you are a competent business manager and well prepared. This thorough preparation makes it easier for the loan officer to say yes.

Your loan request will be evaluated using the 5 C's of credit:

1) Character—If you are not someone to be trusted, then the bank doesn't want to deal with you, no matter how good the deal is.
2) Capacity—What is your financial strength and track record?
3) Capital—How much of your own money do you have invested?
4) Collateral—What is available to support the primary source of repayment?
5) Conditions—What is the economy doing and how will it affect your company?

The primary source of repayment that will be evaluated is the projected cash flow of your business. However, the banker also wants some form of collateral to support the loan in case the cash flow projections do not materialize. Finally, bankers usually require the business owner to personally guarantee the business loan. The banker wants you to be totally committed to your business and the repayment of the loan being requested.

Working With Your Banker

Some dos and don'ts that can help strengthen the relationship with your bankers:

DO:

1) Make an appointment and allocate enough time.
2) Tell it straight, good and bad.
3) Be prepared.
4) Ask questions if you don't understand something.
5) Have a definite plan but be flexible.
6) Keep your banker informed.
7) Negotiate rates after presenting the loan request.

DON'T:

1) Be impatient.
2) Make promises you can't keep.
3) Ask "how much" you can borrow.
4) Negotiate interest rates over the telephone.
5) Spend the money before you ask for it.
6) Change banks solely for a better interest rate.
7) Ever surprise your banker.

Will following this advice really help? Yes! Banks make money from making good business loans. Bankers and business owners often do not understand the others' needs. The communication process often breaks down because of this lack of understanding. Beginning the process by submitting a well-prepared loan proposal indicates to the banker that you are serious about your business and have carefully identified your financing needs.

Following the advice contained on these two pages will place you in the top five percent of the bank's customers. You will be on your way to forming a good relationship with your banker and obtaining your loan.

Personal Financial Statement

Many financial institutions (banks, etc.) will require information about your personal financial resources. The work sheet on the next page will help you prepare a personal financial statement. This statement should be prepared before putting your personal assets into the business.

Step 1:

Prepare a list of all assets you own, whether these assets are paid for or not. Your market value is the amount you would receive by selling the asset for cash.

Step 2:

Add the column to find Total Assets.

Step 3:

Prepare a list of your liabilities (the money you owe).

Step 4:

Add the column to find Total Liabilities.

Step 5:

Calculate your Net Worth by the following method:
Net Worth = Total Assets - Total Liabilities

Personal Financial Statement

Prepared as of ________________

Assets:

Cash—checking accounts	$__________	
Cash—savings accounts	__________	
Notes (contracts)—owed to you	__________	
Certificates of deposits	__________	
Life insurance (cash value)	__________	
Securities—stocks, bonds	__________	
Real estate (market value)	__________	
Vehicles (market value)	__________	
Individual retirement plans, etc.	__________	
Other assets (specify)	__________	
TOTAL ASSETS		$__________

Liabilities:

Current bills—you owe	$__________	
Mortgages on real estate	__________	
Loans—you owe	__________	
Taxes—you owe	__________	
Other liabilities	__________	
TOTAL LIABILITIES		$__________

Net Worth:

(Total assets minus total liabilities equals net worth) $__________

Bibliography

You may benefit from reading some of the following books. Not all of these books are about business plans. These books may provide you some innovative ideas for improving your business.

Business Plans That Win $$$; Stanley R. Rich and David E. Gumpert
Harper & Row; ISBN: 0-06-091391-6

Competitive Strategy; Michael E. Porter
The Free Press; ISBN: 0-02-025360-8

Growing A Business; Paul Hawken
Simon and Schuster; ISBN: 0-67-167164-2

Innovation and Entrepreneurship; Peter Drucker
Harper & Row; ISBN: 0-06-015428-4

Marketing Without Advertising; Michael Phillips and Salli Rasberry
Nolo Press; ISBN: 0-87337-019-8

Small Time Operator; Bernard Kamoroff, CPA
Bell Springs Publishing; ISBN: 0-917510-06-2

Strategic Planning in the Small Business; Charles R. Stoner and Fred L. Fry
South-Western Publishing Co.; ISBN: 0-538-07060-9

Tax Guide For Small Business; Internal Revenue Service
Internal Revenue Service; Publication 334

Beyond Entrepreneurship; James C. Collins and William C. Lazier
Prentice Hall; ISBN: 0-13-085366-6

Visionary Leadership; Bert Nanus
Jossey-Bass; ISBN: 1-55542-460-0

Future Edge; Joel Barker
William Morrow and Company, Inc.; ISBN: 0-688-10936-5

Order Form

Other workbooks prepared by the Oregon Small Business Development Center Network to assist small business owners and potential owners include:

Your Marketing Plan - This workbook helps the small business manager identify and target the potential and actual markets for their goods or services. Fundamental marketing concepts are discussed, and a self-guided format assists the small business manager in developing a working marketing plan. Specific strategies for advertising, public relations and promotions are discussed, with worksheets that help the small business manager plan media efforts and sales strategies.

Your International Business Plan provides a method that small business owners can use to expand their business into international markets. This workbook helps managers evaluate the potential for success in other markets. It serves as a tool to help prepare an organized plan to reach untapped markets.

Su Plan de Negocio - Hispanic small business owners are among the fastest growing segment of our economy. *Su Plan de Negocio* is the Spanish version of *Your Business Plan*, and was translated to help Hispanic entrepreneurs develop their small business and ensure greater success and profitability.

Books may be ordered from: Oregon Small Business Development Center Network
44 West Broadway, Suite 501
Eugene, OR 97401-3021 (541) 726-2250

ORDER FORM

TITLE	QTY	PRICE	TOTAL
Your Business Plan	______	$20.00	$ ______
Your Marketing Plan	______	$20.00	$ ______
Su Plan de Negocio	______	$20.00	$ ______
Your International Business Plan	______	$20.00	$ ______
Please add postage & handling: 1-5 books $5.00; 6-49 books $10.00; Box of 50 $7.50			$ ______
TOTAL	______		$ ______

NAME: ______________________________

ORGANIZATION: ______________________________

ADDRESS: ______________________________

CITY/STATE: ______________________________

P.O. # ____________________ PHONE: ____________________

(Make check payable to: OSBDCN/LCC)